Sebastian Bach
The Boy from Thuringia
Study Guide

By Judy Wilcox

Zeezok publishing

Elyria, OH

Sebastian Bach
The Boy from Thuringia
Study Guide

ISBN 0-9746505-2-8
© 2005 by Zeezok Publishing

Published by:
Zeezok Publishing
PO Box 1960
Elyria, OH 44036

www.Zeezok.com
1-800-749-1681

Map of the major cities Bach visited

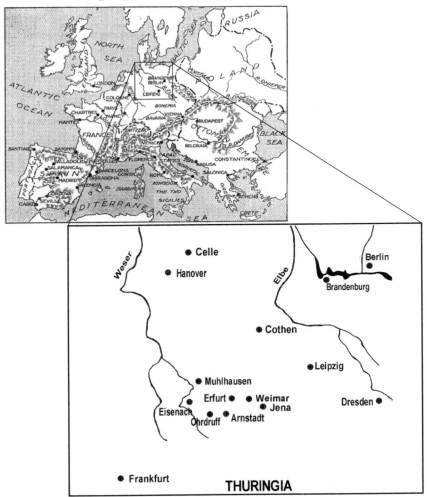

Bach's World and Place in Musical History

Middle Ages	450 – 1450
Renaissance	1450 – 1600
Baroque (J.S. Bach 1685 – 1750)	**1600 – 1750**
Classical	1750 – 1820
Romantic	1820 – 1900
20th Century or New Music	1900 – Present

1685 – 1700

1685 — Bach is born in Eisenach, Germany (March 21, the first day of spring).[1] He is christened two days later on March 23. George Frideric Handel of Germany and Domenico Scarlatti of Italy are also born this year.

Halley draws the first meteorological map. **1686**

1689 — Peter the Great becomes Czar of Russia.

Massachusetts absorbs Plymouth Colony and is given a new charter. **1691**

1694 — Bach's mother, Elisabeth Lämmerhirt, dies.

Bach's father, Johann Ambrosius, dies, and Sebastian moves in with Christoph (his brother) in Ohrdruff. **1695**

1696 – 1700 — Bach attends the Lyceum, a school in Ohrdruff.

The Court of Versailles in France becomes the model for other European courts. **1697**

1698 — Paper manufacturing begins in North America.

A crown treaty is established between the Emperor Leopold I and Frederick III, Elector of Brandenburg. Unmarried women are taxed in Berlin. John Wesley, the preacher, is born. **1700**

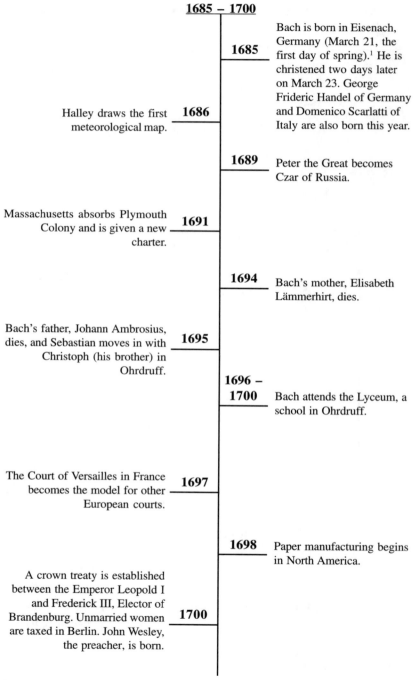

Chapter I – In the Thuringian Village of Eisenach

Reading Comprehension Questions

1. What talent did nearly all members of the Bach family seem to share?
   • A talent for music, or musical ability, p. 11.
2. Sebastian's father taught him about his great-great-grandfather, Veit Bach, who took his lute with him to work. Do you remember what his occupation was?
   • A miller, p. 13.
3. The Bach family did something annually. What was it, and why did the whole village of Eisenach enjoy it?
   • They had a family reunion, and it was a musical feast for the village as well as the family, pp. 14, 18.
4. Sebastian sang in a scholars' choir that sang the same songs as an important Reformation leader in church history. Can you think of his name?
   • Martin Luther, p. 20.
5. What sad events changed Sebastian's life when he was a young boy?
   • His parents died, p. 20.
6. Sebastian went to live with his brother Christoph, but Christoph was very strict about something. What were his rules, and how did Sebastian respond to them?
   • His rules were to not practice on the clavier for more than an hour a day, and to not use the music books from his library. Sebastian responded by sneaking into the library, taking the book to his room, and copying the music for himself at night, pp. 21–24.
7. In spite of Christoph's confiscation of Sebastian's copy of the music, Sebastian had done something remarkable in the six-month process. What was it?
   • He had memorized the music of the masters he was copying, p. 28.
8. As the chapter ends, where is Sebastian preparing to go?
   • Choir school at St. Michael's in Lüneburg, p. 29.

Character Qualities

Hospitality (pp. 14–15) – The Bach family was known as a hospitable family. Hospitality means being friendly and generous in entertaining guests and visitors. The family reunion was just one example of the Bach hospitality in action. It was a quality that Sebastian maintained throughout his life (p. 126).

Family-Oriented (pp. 12, 14–15) – Again, the reunion attests to the importance of family in the Bach household. The very fact that Ambrosius took time to teach Sebastian how to play the violin also shows the significance of family unity and activity. This trait is something that Sebastian learned well from his father because he acted in the same manner with his own family (p. 105).

Sense of Humor and Wit – Sebastian himself was known as "a merry and companionable fellow."[2] In this chapter, the portion about the quodlibet of the fat cow that would not go to pasture and the quiet flowing river (pp. 15–16) hints at Sebastian's love for laughter and merry songs.

Industriousness (pp. 23–24) – Sebastian was not afraid of being constantly or regularly occupied, of keeping busy. In this chapter, we see that busyness at an early age when Sebastian was willing to sacrifice sleep for the sake of copying Christoph's manuscripts by moonlight. Sebastian was also unafraid of a two-

hundred mile hike to St. Michael's in Lüneburg in order to attend choir school. Now if that's not industriousness, then it is at least a fantastic exercise routine!

Tidbits of Interest

Pages 9, 11 – Eisenach (pronounced \eye-zen-ahk\), the village, nestles on the edge of the Thuringian forest. It is also the location of Wartburg Castle, where Martin Luther (1483–1546) once sought refuge from Pope Leo X and other critics from the Roman Catholic Church. Wartburg Castle is where Luther translated the New Testament into German, making it available to the common man for study and meditation. Remember that Luther emphasized having a personal, living, Bible-based faith in Jesus Christ. He was himself a musician, declaring that music was second unto the Gospel itself, so that many of the hymns from the Lutheran hymnal became a source of stimulation for Bach's works.[3] In Eisenach, Bach sang in the scholars' choir, which was an all-boy choir in which boys sang even the soprano parts. Often, they sang chorales, which were German Lutheran hymn-tunes, many composed or arranged by Luther himself.

Page 9 – Thuringia (pronounced \th(y)u-rin-jeeh\) is the most westerly of the old East German states. It includes wooded heights and slate mountains. It remained Sebastian's favorite region to visit (p. 114).

Page 11 – St. George's Church in Eisenach is a Lutheran church where, at each christening, families are still informed that Johann Sebastian Bach was once christened in the same sanctuary. Christening is the ceremony of baptizing and naming a baby.

Page 11 – Sebastian is the name Bach is called most frequently in Wheeler and Deucher's book. There were 53 individuals in the Bach family who were named Johann.[4] Oh, and five of his own sons were named Johann, and two of his daughters were named Johanna![5] So you can see why children were often called by their middle names to eliminate some confusion.

Page 13 – Veit (also known as Vitus), Sebastian's great-great-grandfather, appears to have been compelled to escape persecution in Hungary for his Lutheran faith.[6] Music was passed down from father to child in the Bach family. Veit taught his son Hans, who taught Christoph, who taught Ambrosius, who taught Sebastian.[7] Veit took a lute to the mill with him. It is a stringed instrument with a large pear-shaped body, a long neck with a fretted fingerboard, and a head with tuning pegs.

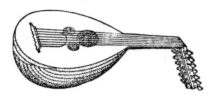

Page 13 – A clavichord is a small, early keyboard instrument with hammer action. Strings are struck by a tangent (a small oblong strip of metal), which elicits soft sounds from the strings. It is limited in its range in terms of dynamics (loudness and softness). Sebastian's son, C.P.E. Bach, became a leading player of the clavichord in the 18th century.

Pages 14, 15 – The Bach family was wonderfully musical. In fact, one author says that Bach's "is the largest family tree in music."[8] There are more than 50 musicians with the name of Bach who are recognized by musicologists. It is interesting that the word *bach* in German means *brook*. Ludwig Beethoven once exclaimed, "His name ought not to be Bach, but ocean, because of his infinite and inexhaustible wealth of combinations and harmonies."[9] Even the letters of their surname — B-A-C-H — spell out a melodic succession.[10] In German, the musical note B actually represents B-flat, while B natural was indicated occasionally by the letter H. So Bach's name in musical notes was B-flat, A, C, and B natural.[11]

Page 15 – Quodlibets were two different songs sung at the same time. In this story a song about a cow and a river are sung during the family reunion. Quodlibet (pronounced \quahd-leh-bet\)

comes from the Latin term meaning "what you please." Usually it is a lighthearted composition containing a combination of well-known tunes. Bach's later *Goldberg Variations* were quodlibets combining the theme of the variations with two popular songs of the time.

Page 20 – Johann Christoph Bach, Sebastian's older brother by fourteen years, was the church organist in Ohrdruff who gave Sebastian his first keyboard lessons and took responsibility for him in 1695, after their father's death. Christoph had been a student of the composer Johann Pachelbel.[12] His library of music contained French and Italian manuscripts by the best Italian and French composers of the time.[13] It is believed that the copying of the works of the masters by moonlight may have contributed to Sebastian's blindness by age 65.

Page 21 – A clavier is the keyboard of a musical instrument. In some cases, it refers to a particular early keyboard instrument. The first piano is believed to have been invented in Italy in 1709. Pianos were not common instruments until the late 18th century.

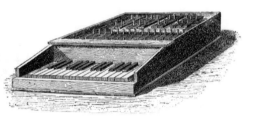

Pages 20, 29 – The Lyceum was similar to a high school. He attended school there from 1696 to 1700, ending school in second place among his classmates. Students read the classical poets, and learned Latin, Greek, theology, rhetoric, logic, history, geography, and music there.

Page 29 – Wheeler and Deucher state that Sebastian was going to St. Michael's to study music, but it is also true that Sebastian's insufficient funds made him ineligible to continue attending school at the Lyceum.[14] Sebastian's friend in school and on his adventure to Lüneburg was Georg Erdmann. Erdmann later became the Imperial Russian Resident Agent in Danzig, Prussia (now Poland).

1700 – 1703

**1700 –
1702** Bach attends school at St. Michael's in Lüneburg. He learns musical composition and organ playing at St. Michael's.

"Captain" William Kidd is hanged for piracy. Elector Frederick III of Brandenburg crowns himself King Frederick I of Prussia. **1701**

1702 William III dies in England and is succeeded by Queen Anne. She also gives royal approval to horseracing, and originates the sweepstakes idea.

**1702 –
1703** Bach plays violin in the Duke's court orchestra at Weimar.

1703 Isaac Newton is elected President of the Royal Society. Also, Peter the Great lays the foundations of St. Petersburg, Russia.

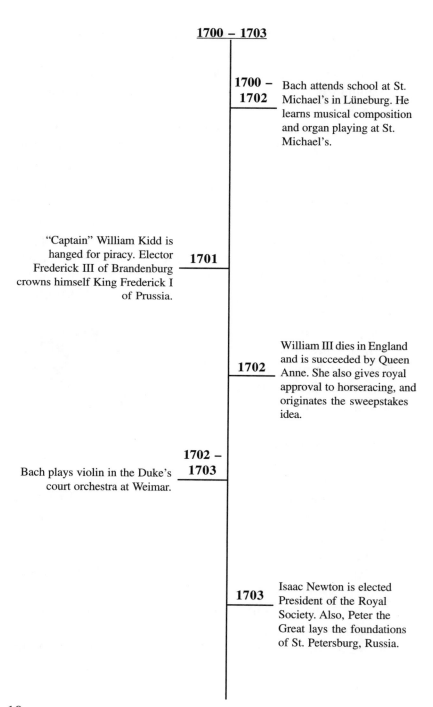

10

Chapter II – At St. Michael's in Lüneburg

Reading Comprehension Questions

1. List some ways that people showed kindness or helpfulness to Sebastian and Erdmann in the beginning of this chapter.
   • A man gave them a wagon ride, p. 35; others gave them directions to St. Michael's, p. 37; they received food from the monk, p. 38.

2. The boys were excited about studying music to their heart's content (p. 39). Initially, what was Sebastian's favorite instrument to play, and how did he improve the playing of it?
   • The clavier, and he improved the playing of it by using all five fingers, not just the three middle fingers, p. 40.

3. Sebastian was then allowed to play on another instrument, and received lessons from Herr Böhm of St. John's Church. What was the instrument?
   • The organ, p. 42.

4. After three years at the school, Sebastian's high soprano voice changed, and he was not needed in the choir. How did he pay for his lodging at school?
   • He played in the church orchestra and accompanied singers, p. 45.

5. Why did Sebastian walk to Hamburg?
   • No, not for a hamburger. He went to hear the organ master Reinken, p. 46.

6. After the concert and on his journey back to Lüneburg, Sebastian's mind was filled with thoughts of what?
   • Thoughts of music, p. 51. I suppose thoughts of food would be an acceptable response, too, p. 52.

7. How did Sebastian receive money to buy his dinner on his trip back to Lüneburg?
   • Two herrings' heads, each with a gold ducat, were dropped out a window right near Sebastian, p. 52.

8. Sebastian received an invitation from the Duke of Weimar. What was he to do?
   • Live at the Duke's palace and play in his orchestra, p. 55.

Character Qualities

Humility – Sebastian was willing to sleep in a hayloft (p. 36) in order to make it to St. Michael's, and in a cattle stall (p. 49) in order to hear Reinken play the organ in Hamburg. He also recognized the need to change his service at the school when his soprano voice changed (p. 45), so he began playing in the church orchestra and accompanying singers as needed.

Wit and Sense of Humor (p. 52) – You have to admit that finding gold coins in herrings' mouths is somewhat humorous (providentially so). Anyone who likes coffee will be delighted to learn that Bach also loved coffee and even wrote a cantata about it (*The Coffee Cantata*)! That's good caffeinated humor in its richest sense. Once when Bach was praised for his skill as an organist, he replied, "There is nothing wonderful about it. You have only to hit the right notes at the right moment and the instrument does the rest."[15]

Industriousness – Bach's development of new fingering techniques for the clavier (p. 40) and his willingness to walk all the way to Hamburg for an organ concert (p. 46) both attest to his willingness to work and sacrifice for his music.

Tidbits of Interest

Page 33 – Lüneburg (pronounced \loo-neh-burg\) is a city in the Saxony region of Germany. It is not as mountainous a region as Thuringia.

Page 34 – You may want to try the following recipe for rye or black bread…. Let your students enjoy a slice while you read this chapter. It will bring the story more to life for them and fill their bellies with healthy, warm, chocolaty food.

German Rye Bread

3 c. all-purpose flour
1/4 c. unsweetened cocoa powder
2 pkg. active dry yeast
1 tbsp. caraway seed
1 tbsp. salt
1/3 c. molasses
2 tbsp. butter
1 tbsp. sugar
3-1/2 c. rye flour
Cooking oil

In a large bowl, combine all-purpose flour, cocoa, yeast, and caraway seed. Heat and stir molasses, butter, sugar, 2 c. water, and 2 tbsp. oil until warm. Add to dry mixture. Beat at low speed with electric mixer for 1 to 2 minutes, scraping the bowl. Beat 3 minutes at high speed. Then by hand, stir in enough rye flour to make a soft dough. Turn out onto lightly floured surface; knead till smooth (about 5 minutes). Cover; let rest 20 minutes. Punch down. Divide in half. Shape into 2 round loaves on greased baking sheets or in 2 greased, 8-inch pie plates. Brush with a small amount of cooking oil. Slash tops with knife. Cover; let rise until double (45 to 60 minutes). Bake at 400 degrees for 25 to 30 minutes. Remove from pans; cool. Makes 2 loaves.

Page 37 – Do you know why the cap and lantern of the church at St. Michael's was of green copper? It was caused by oxidation, which is a reaction in which oxygen combines chemically with another substance. Copper almost always turns green or greenish-blue when it is exposed to the outside elements, such as rain and snow. It is the nature of

copper and bronze to protect itself by forming this greenish "patina" on itself to prevent rusting and corrosion. Your children can see the same process by putting a copper penny outside for a while. Oxidation also explains the greenish-blue color of the metal on the Statue of Liberty, for example.

Page 40 – Sebastian spent hours practicing on the clavier and experimenting with new fingering techniques. He is said to have had large hands that could stretch across 12 notes while performing running passages with his three middle fingers.[16] This was "an almost unheard of departure from the conventional way of playing scales. And with what amazing results!"[17]

Page 41 – The organ is a keyboard instrument in which sound is produced by air passing through pipes of various size and construction to give a wide variety of pitches and timbres. In Bach's time, bellows attached to foot pedals were the means of forcing air through the pipes of the organ. It seems that all the miles of walking that Sebastian did helped build up his leg muscles, allowing him to pump the organ pedals all the more effectively. He also used a stick in his mouth to allow him to reach certain notes he couldn't have otherwise reached with his hands.[18] The organ is sometimes referred to as "the king of instruments." Bach was actually better known in his day as an *organist* than as a *composer*! Only ten of his compositions were published in his lifetime, though he wrote more than one thousand works

(three-quarters of which were for Christian worship services).

Page 42 – The first person to give Sebastian organ lessons was Herr (Mr.) Georg Böhm, the organist of St. John's Church in Lüneburg. He soon taught Sebastian all that he could, so Sebastian progressed on his own, finding the most difficult music he could and composing pieces of his own.

Page 43 – A minuet is a triple-meter (three beats per measure) French dance that was popular from the mid-17th century to the end of the 18th century. It also appears as an occasional element of the baroque instrumental suite.

Page 46 – In his efforts to become a better organist, and in his passion for lovely music, Sebastian hiked to Hamburg to hear Jan Adams Reinken, the organ master at St. Katherine's. This was a thirty-mile hike. Reinken was a man in his eighties at that point, but his mastery awed and inspired the budding composer in Bach.

Page 52 – God's providential care for Bach on his return trip to Lüneburg is remarkable. The two gold ducats in the two herring heads were gold coins used in various European countries; these were apparently Danish coins.[19] According to one anecdotal telling of this event, Bach "had hardly started to tear [the herring heads] apart when he found a Danish ducat hidden in each head. This find enabled him not only to add a portion of roast meat to his meal but also at the first opportunity to make another pilgrimage, in greater comfort, to Mr. Reinecke [Reinken] in Hamburg."[20]

Page 55 – Sebastian received an invitation from the Duke of Weimar, which is a city in central Germany on the Lim River in the Thuringian region. Sebastian was to play in the Duke's court orchestra. The Duke of Weimar at this time was Wilhelm Ernst, who was known as a connoisseur and lover of music.[21]

1703 – 1717

Bach tests a new organ at New Church in Arnstadt and is offered the post of church organist almost immediately. He ministers there for four years.

1703

1704 Bach writes his first cantata.

Bach walks two hundred miles to Lübeck to hear Dietrich Buxtehude, the greatest organist of his generation.

1705

Bach returns to Arnstadt (after being away for several months in Lübeck).

1706 Benjamin Franklin is born this year. Johann Pachelbel, the German organist and composer, dies.

Bach becomes the organist in St. Blasius Church in Mühlhausen. He also marries Maria Barbara in October. The organist Dietrich Buxtehude dies. Handel meets Scarlatti in Venice. Mount Fuji erupts for the last time (so far). Scotland and England unite under the name Great Britain.

1707

1708 – 1717 Bach returns to the court of the Duke of Saxe-Weimar where he serves as chamber musician, concertmaster, and organist.

1708 Bach's first child, Catherina Dorothea, is born.

The pianoforte (piano) is invented by the Italian harpsichord maker, Bartolomeo Cristofori.

1709

1710 Bach's son, Wilhelm Friedemann, is born. Handel goes to England.

A clarinet is used for the first time in an orchestra in an opera by J.A. Hasse.

1711

1712 Future Frederick the Great, King of Prussia, is born. St. Petersburg becomes the capital of Russia (until 1922).

King Frederick I of Prussia dies and is succeeded by Frederick William I (who rules until 1740).

1713

1714 Bach's son, Carl Philipp Emanuel Bach, is born. Queen Anne dies and is succeeded by George Louis, elector of Hanover (for whom Handel is court music director); he becomes King George I.

Chapter III – Sebastian's Many Journeys

Reading Comprehension Questions

1. What instrument did Sebastian play in the Duke's orchestra?
   • Violin, p. 62.
2. Sebastian visited family in Arnstadt. While there, he was invited to try a new item in the church. What was it?
   • An organ, p. 68.
3. After the organ concert at the church, what did the church leaders ask him to do?
   • Become the church organist and choir director, p. 69.
4. Do you remember some of the elements of Sebastian's vow to the church leaders before beginning his duties there?
   • He promised to be a faithful servant of God, a good organist, to carry out all his duties, and to obey the church leaders' wishes, p. 70.
5. Sebastian loved that there was time to compose organ music at the church in Arnstadt, but how did the church leaders respond to his works?
   • They complained that they were too long and not rehearsed enough. They were difficult to sing along with because they were sometimes improvisational, p. 72.
6. Sebastian asked permission to see the great organist, Buxtehude, in Lübeck — but only for four weeks. How long did Sebastian end up staying?
   • Three months, p. 74.
7. What did the Duke of Weimar ask Sebastian to do?
   • Live with him again and be the court organist, p. 79.
8. Who was considered the only other German composer equal to Bach?
   • Handel, who had moved to England, p. 80.
9. What competition had been arranged at the end of this chapter?
   • A contest between Bach and Marchand to see who was the better keyboard player, p. 82.

Character Qualities

Integrity (p. 70) – Bach asked the Duke of Weimar for permission to leave his role in the court orchestra before taking the position of organist at New Church in Arnstadt. Bach agreed to take certain vows regarding his duties in New Church, and he lived up to those vows for four years, even though he sometimes found the responsibilities constricting and suffocating.

Industriousness (p. 72) – Again, Bach was willing to walk many miles to hear music by a master when he walked two hundred miles to Lübeck to hear Buxtehude. He served for nine years under the Duke, and not just in a musical capacity. That he would be willing to work as a footman and a huntsman says something about Bach's work ethic (p. 80).

Faith (p. 76) – He was willing to serve in the church, even taking part of his pay in the form of corn, wood, and fish. A substantial portion of his musical works focused on biblical themes. In some regards, Bach desired a position as a church organist so that he could spend more time composing, because he believed that the "object of all music should be the glory of God."[22]

Tidbits of Interest

Page 60 – There are a couple of composition styles mentioned in this chapter. A gavotte (pronounced \geh-vaht\) is a French peasant dance that is marked by the raising of one's feet. The tune is usually in moderately quick 4/4 time.

Page 63 – Both men and women wore wigs during this time. It was apparently a sign of maturing from boyhood to manhood, as well as an accessory of fashion.[23] Manufactured head coverings were typically of real hair during the 17th and 18th centuries, and men's wigs became common in those centuries. Bach still wore plain clothing, but he is often seen with a white wig in portraits and paintings from that time.

Page 66 – A polonaise (pronounced \pahl-eh-nayz\) is a solemn processional, or a Polish dance in triple meter. Chopin actually became best known for this style of composition in his piano works.

18

Page 68 – During holiday from responsibilities at the Duke's, Bach visited family in Arnstadt (pronounced \arn-shtat\), a town known as "the Gateway to the Thuringian Forest." While he was there, his family invited him to try the new organ at New Church in Arnstadt. Bach loved to "test the lungs" of new organs by pulling out all the stops — giving full air to all the pipes.[24] An organist at that time would provide accompaniment for church services, improvise preludes and other needed incidental music, and test new organs as needed. Bach accepted the position and began composing in earnest — particularly works that led others in glorifying God. In fact, biographers consistently note that the "focus of his emotional life was undoubtedly in religion, and in the service of religion through music." [25]

Page 72 – Bach served in New Church for four years; however, the members were Pietists who saw little room for creativity in art, so they were displeased by Bach's fanciful preludes. He was even criticized for sometimes startling the congregation by using unusual sounds on the organ.[26] So his two hundred mile hike to Lübeck to hear the greatest organist of his time, Dietrich Buxtehude (pronounced \boox-teh-hoo-deh\), may have been a much-needed musical respite. Buxtehude was a Danish-German composer who remained the appointed organist at St. Mary's Church in Lübeck for nearly forty years. He reinstated the

tradition of *Abendmusik*, which was an annual series of church concerts, occurring at Christmas time. (This would explain Bach's having to trudge through great drifts of snow on his return to Arnstadt, p. 74.) Bach was so moved and edified by Buxtehude's music that he is said to have imitated and perfected it.[27]

Page 77 – Bach's months at St. Blasius Church in Mühlhausen (pronounced \myool-haw-zen\) were pleasant. It was there that Bach solidified his purpose for music. In 1708 he wrote that he desired to create "well-regulated church music to the glory of God."[28] Bach often initialed blank manuscript pages with the letters "J.J." meaning *Jesu Juva* ("Help me, Jesus") or "I.N.J." meaning *In Nomine Jesu* ("In the name of Jesus"). Frequently his compositions were initialed at the end with the letters "S.D.G." representing *Soli Deo Gloria* or "To God alone, the glory."[29] Once he wrote, "Where there is devotional music, God is always at hand with His gracious presence."[30] (This comment was written in response to his reading of 2 Chronicles 5:13.)

He had no compunction about composing works that followed the established "rules" of music from the Baroque period. In fact, he preferred the traditional ways of composing, not changing the music fashions of the time.[31] Baroque music is contrapuntal in style; that is, several independent voices are used to weave a tapestry of sound. Some writers claim that the Baroque period was in response to the wars of the Renaissance and Reformation that had devastated much of Europe (1450–1600). Artists, architects, and musicians were attempting to escape the harsh realities by creating an ideal world through their arts. Other Baroque contemporaries of Bach's were the composers Vivaldi, Rameau, and Handel. Artists from this period included masters such as Rembrandt, Rubens, Velazquez, and Bernini.

Page 77 – Maria Barbara Bach was a second cousin of Sebastian's, so she was one of the musical Bachs. She and Sebastian had seven children, three of whom died in childhood. Two of their children, Wilhelm Friedemann and Carl Philipp Emanuel, later became musicians in their own rights.[32]

Page 78 – The harpsichord was one instrument Bach began to play more frequently. It is a keyboard instrument with strings running from front to back of its wing-shaped horizontal box and soundboard. However, a mechanism is used to pluck the strings, rather than a hammer-like mechanism to strike each string. Dynamic variations can be achieved by using stops that activate different lengths of string, and by using a muting buff stop.

Page 80 – When the Duke of Weimar extended another opportunity to play for his court, Bach accepted the invitation and moved his new wife, Maria Barbara, to the Duke's palace. He served the Duke for nine years — not only as musician, but also as footman (the servant in the livery, attending a rider or running in front of his master's carriage, or serving at the table, tending the door, and running errands) and as a huntsman (managing a hunt and looking after the hounds).

Page 80 – Sebastian was becoming more renowned throughout the region for his skill on the keyboard. Only George Frideric Handel is considered to have been the equal of Bach in terms of musical composition and mastery. Handel was born the same year as Bach, but he was born in Halle, Germany, and he studied in Hamburg. He moved to England in 1711 and lived there for the remainder of his life, dying in 1759. (Bach never once traveled outside of Germany, by the way.)

Page 81 – A musette (pronounced \myoo-zet\) is a small bagpipe having a soft, sweet tone, or a piece named after that instrument. It is also a small knapsack with a shoulder strap for carrying provisions and personal belongings. It only seems appropriate that a man who hiked so much of his life would write such a work.

Page 82 – In the early 18th century, Germany was divided into hundreds of small states and imperial districts. There were over 300 such regions during Bach's lifetime. Prussia was the powerful state and former kingdom in northeast Germany, bordering the Baltic Sea, which was ruled by the Hohenzollern family. When Germany became a single country, the Prussian royal family ruled as emperors.[33] It continued as a state within the German nation until 1977.

Wheeler and Deucher refer to the King of Prussia as Ferdinand Augustus. However, in researching the names of the Prussian kings from this time, the king was Frederick William I, known as "the Soldier King," who reigned from 1713–1740. No person named Ferdinand Augustus is ever listed as a king of any German kingdom.

1717

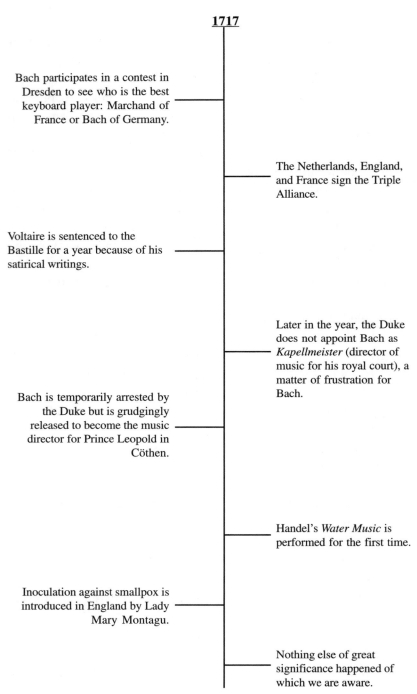

Bach participates in a contest in Dresden to see who is the best keyboard player: Marchand of France or Bach of Germany.

The Netherlands, England, and France sign the Triple Alliance.

Voltaire is sentenced to the Bastille for a year because of his satirical writings.

Later in the year, the Duke does not appoint Bach as *Kapellmeister* (director of music for his royal court), a matter of frustration for Bach.

Bach is temporarily arrested by the Duke but is grudgingly released to become the music director for Prince Leopold in Cöthen.

Handel's *Water Music* is performed for the first time.

Inoculation against smallpox is introduced in England by Lady Mary Montagu.

Nothing else of great significance happened of which we are aware.

Chapter IV– The Contest with Marchand

Reading Comprehension Questions

1. How do Marchand and Sebastian seem to be different in this chapter, and can you provide some examples that show these differences?
   • Marchand was from France, p. 85; he seemed proud, p. 85; he wore fancy clothes, p. 85; he focused on his own compositions, p. 85; he was somewhat cowardly, leaving the contest early, p. 89. Bach was from Germany, p. 85; he acted humbly and wore simple clothes, p. 88; he asked the king for a musical idea for a fugue, p. 86; and he showed strength of character in not mocking Marchand for leaving, p. 90.

2. On the day of the competition, when it was Marchand's turn to perform, what announcement was made?
   • Marchand had left town in a carriage, p. 89.

3. Who asked Bach to become his court organist and violinist, and why did Bach agree to come?
   • Prince Leopold of Cöthen, and Bach accepted because the Prince loved music too, pp. 90-91.

Character Qualities

Humility (p. 88) – Bach came to the competition dressed in a plain black suit. He did not mock Marchand for leaving before the contest was completed (p. 90).

Creativity (p. 86) – He asked the King for a melody, and from that tune he improvised an entire fugue, weaving the melody in and out. Moreover, he accomplished such a feat in front of a live and musically critical audience!

Tidbits of Interest

Page 85 – Jean-Baptiste Volumier was the *Kapellmeister* for Dresden, and he was the one who coordinated the contest between Bach and Marchand. Jean Louis Marchand (pronounced \zhan loo-ee mar-shawn\ – with a very nasal ending) was the private organist of the King of France (King Louis XV). Marchand was apparently applying for the post of organist at the court of Dresden. Volumier was not thrilled with the prospect of Marchand getting the job, so he arranged for his German friend to challenge the Frenchman. A contemporary of Bach's wrote in a letter in 1788 regarding this competition: "Perhaps it will be concluded that Bach was a challenging musical braggart...No, Bach was anything but proud of his qualities and never let anyone feel his superiority. On the contrary, he was uncommonly modest, tolerant, and very polite to other musicians. The affair with Marchand became known mainly through others; he himself told the story but seldom, and then only when he was urged."[34]

Page 86 – A fugue (pronounced \fewg\) is a musical piece that uses certain rules to dictate the structure of the interaction of polyphonic voices, yet skill allows the exhibition of creative invention. This "freedom within an ordered world" concept mirrors Bach's lifestyle in the midst of the Baroque period, doesn't it?

Page 87 – The Marshal, Count Flemming, provided the home for the contest. He is also referred to as the Prime Minister who so loved music that he supported his own orchestra in his private residence.[35] He even bought a new harpsichord for the contest. The Crown Prince mentioned in this chapter is Frederick II, who later became the greatest King of Prussia (even calling himself such: Frederick the Great). While "the Soldier King" Frederick William I was not fond of music, science, or anything French, his oldest son was exactly the opposite — enjoying music, admiring French styles and architecture, and pursuing studies beyond mere military concerns.

Wheeler and Deucher make no mention of this event in Bach's life, but Bach *was* imprisoned for a time. Bach's most important duty in the Duke's court remained writing music, which was played and sung in the court chapel. Yet, when the position of *Kapellmeister* for the Duke became available, the Duke appointed a less qualified individual, and Bach was upset.[36] He determined to accept Prince Leopold's request to play at his court in Cöthen. However, the Duke was angered by Bach's move to a higher position, so the Duke put Bach in prison for a month. Bach made good use of his time, nonetheless. He wrote 46 pieces of music,[37] and composed a substantial portion of his *Orgelbüchlein* ("Little Book for the Organ") during that month.[38]

1717 – 1750

1717 –
1723

Bach serves as court conductor for Prince Leopold.

1718 Peter the Great murders his son and heir, Alexis. England declares war on Spain.

Bach marries Anna Magdalena Wülcken and composes the *Brandenburg Concertos*. Peter the Great is proclaimed Emperor of All the Russias.

1721

1722 The first part of the *Well-Tempered Clavier* and Bach's first music book for Anna Magadalena are composed. Organ master Reinken dies.

Bach becomes the cantor at St. Thomas's School in Leipzig.

1723

1729 Bach's *St. Matthew Passion* is performed for the first time.

Bach's son, Johann Christoph Friedrich, is born.

1732

1735 Bach's youngest son, Johann Christian, is born.

Bach is given the title of royal court composer by the Elector of Saxony, Frederick Augustus II, also known as Frederick the Great.

1736

1737 Antonio Stradivari, of violin fame, dies.

The future King George III is born.

1738

1740 Bach's second son enters the service of Frederick II. Bach's eyesight is now very poor.

Antonio Vivaldi of Italy dies.

1741

1742 Bach composes the *Goldberg Variations*. Handel's *Messiah* is first performed in Dublin.

Bach's first grandson, Johann August, son of C.P.E. Bach, is born.

1745

1747 Bach visits Frederick the Great's court in Potsdam.

Bach has two unsuccessful eye surgeries in March and April, leaving him almost blind. He dies in Leipzig on July 28 at age 65.

1750

26

Chapter V – The Home of the Bachs

Reading Comprehension Questions

1. How did Bach sometimes help Prince Leopold in matters beyond music?
   - The Prince asked his advice on royal matters, p. 99.

2. In Hamburg, after Sebastian had given an organ concert, the organ master Reinken told Bach that he alone had "the power to make it speak." Was this high praise? Why or why not?
   - Yes, it was coming from a great organist who appreciated the power and effectiveness of Bach's compositions, p. 101.

3. What was an advantage for the Bach family in having Sebastian become the cantor at St. Thomas's School in Leipzig (instead of remaining with Prince Leopold)?
   - Friedemann and Emanuel, Bach's sons, would receive a fine education, p. 104.

4. Bach's family experienced tragedy in this chapter (though it was only given one sentence), followed by a new joy. What were those events?
   - Maria Barbara's death and Magdalena as Bach's new and musical wife, p. 105.

5. If asked to prove that Bach loved children, what evidence could you supply?
   - He had twenty of them! He taught them to play instruments and read music, p. 105. He wrote music for them, p. 106. He played with them — games, teasing, tickling, etc., p. 110. He took them with him on trips occasionally, p. 100. He led them in prayers, p. 110.

6. For whom did Emanuel become the Court Musician? Hint: He was the same character for whom "Old Bach" played on seven harpsichords and composed a fugue on the spur of the moment.
   - King Frederick the Great, p. 115.

7. How is Johann Sebastian Bach's music like a ray of light?
   • His music opened or made visible the path of music for later musicians, p. 126. He often wrote of biblical themes, so his music can also enlighten us spiritually.

Character Qualities

Family-Oriented (pp. 105–111) – Again, doesn't the fact that he had twenty children speak volumes? He played with his children (p. 110), cuddled them when they were crying (p. 111), wrote music for them (p. 106), and led them in their prayers (p. 110).

Faith – His cantatas emphasize the words and the message of the gospel.[39] His last work, dictated from his bed, was a chorale entitled *Before Thy Throne I Come*.

Integrity (p. 104)– For the sake of his sons' educations, he chose the position of cantor over staying in a relative life of luxury with the Prince.

Hospitality and Generosity (p. 121) – His home was recognized as one of graciousness, friendship, and love.

Industriousness – In his lifetime, Bach wrote three hundred cantatas (only two hundred of which survived), five passions, several masses, three oratorios, and instrumental music primarily for church worship. In his own words, he believed that any "devout man could do as much as I have done, if he worked as hard."[40]

Tidbits of Interest

Page 98 – Bach was identified with the Calvinist Reformed Church when he was court conductor for the Prince of Cöthen, but he felt constricted by the Calvinist view that artistic music had no place in the church, and that artists should not depict biblical scenes.[41] This time of service became known as Bach's orchestral and chamber music period.[42]

Page 99 – Prince Leopold was himself a gifted musician of the viola, violin, and harpsichord, so he enjoyed having his music master travel with him. In 1720, Bach returned from a musical tour with the Prince to discover that Maria Barbara had died and was already buried (p. 105). He "had left her hale and hearty on his departure. The news that she had been ill and died reached him only when he entered his own house."[43] Unfortunately, or perhaps providentially, Prince Leopold married Frederica Henrietta, a woman who was not interested in music. She resented her husband's practicing and made life difficult for Bach.[44] Her actions may have encouraged his decision to take the role of cantor for St. Thomas's Church in Leipzig in 1723.

Page 102 – A gigue (pronounced \geeg\) is a jolly jig, or a rapid dance normally in compound duple meter (meaning the main beats are divided into three rather than two). It became the accepted final dance in the baroque instrumental suite.

Page 104 – As cantor at St. Thomas's School in Leipzig, Bach was responsible for the musical education of the students at the school, and often for all the other musical activities in the city. This role required him to produce a new composition for each service of the four largest churches in the city.[45] Moving away from the Prince's court lowered his social status and salary, but this new role allowed him to stay home so that he could focus on composing.[46] These were his crowning years of creativity, and he wrote vast numbers of vocal pieces and cantatas while in Leipzig.

Page 105 – He remarried in 1721, taking as his wife a woman twenty years his junior, who was an excellent soprano who could also play the keyboard; her name was Anna Magdalena Wülcken (pronounced \vool-ken\). She gave him 13 more children — although, sadly, seven of them did not survive to adulthood.

Page 107 – A bourrée (pronounced \boo-ray\) is an old French dance of duple rhythm (marked by two or a multiple of two beats per measure of music).

Page 116 – Bach was going to see his first grandchild, the son of C.P.E. Bach (who was the keyboard player in Frederick II's court), when he visited the King in Potsdam.[47] Frederick the

Great was King from 1740 to 1786. Prussia became one of the great states of Europe with vastly expanded territories and impressive military strength under his leadership. Moreover, the King was a gifted amateur musician. Bach improvised on his musical theme at their meeting and improvised a fugue with six parts.[48]

Potsdam was the capital of Brandenburg state and was the royal residence of Prussia's Frederick the Great. Just an aside comment for you history buffs: This *is* the city that became the site of the Potsdam Conference (July 17–August 2, 1945) after Germany's surrender in World War II. Truman, Stalin, and Churchill met to discuss European peace settlements, the occupation of Germany and Austria, reparations, and the continuing war against Japan.

Bach had two eye operations shortly after visiting the King, but these operations weakened him and led to his total blindness before his death. He died in relative obscurity, even being buried in an unmarked grave at St. John's Cemetery in Leipzig. His body was exhumed in 1894, and again in 1950, at which time it was moved to a more esteemed grave at St. Thomas's Church.

Page 120 – During his day, Bach was known as a master of the keyboard instruments — the organ, harpsichord, and clavichord. It wasn't until after his death that his overall musical power became more evident. Bach's compositions influenced later masters such as Mozart, Beethoven, Mendelssohn, Chopin, Schumann, and Brahms.[49] He has been called "The Father of Modern Music."

It seems appropriate that a musician who had such an impact on music and future composers should be known the world over — and even "the solar system over." In fact, in 1977 the *Voyager* spacecraft was launched into our solar system. On it was a gold-plated record on which — among other sounds and compositions — three of Bach's pieces are recorded. The *first* communication on the gold-plated record is Bach's *Brandenburg* Concerto no. 2. Granted, no space alien will ever encounter these compositions, but it is unique to think that the God of the Heavens is glorying in the music that Johann Sebastian Bach lovingly offered Him.

Endnotes

[1] Roland Vernon, *Introducing Bach* (Parsippany, NJ: Simon & Schuster, 1996), 30.

[2] Henry Thomas and Dana Lee Thomas, *Living Biographies of Great Composers* (Garden City, NY: Nelson Doubleday, Inc., 1940), 5.

[3] Jane Stuart Smith and Betty Carlson, *The Gift of Music: Great Composers and Their Influence* (Wheaton, IL: Crossway Books, 1995), 33.

[4] Kathleen Krull, *Lives of the Musicians: Good Times, Bad Times* (San Diego, CA: Harcourt, Inc., 2002), 15.

[5] Ibid., 16.

[6] Karl Geiringer, *Johann Sebastian Bach* (New York, NY: Oxford University Press, 1966), 4.

[7] Jeanette Winter, *Sebastian: A Book about Bach* (San Diego, CA: Harcourt Brace & Company, 1999), 3–4.

[8] Krull, *Lives of the Musicians*, 15.

[9] Patrick Kavanaugh, *Spiritual Lives of the Great Composers* (Grand Rapids, MI: Zondervan, 1996), 19.

[10] Thomas and Thomas, *Living Biographies of Great Composers*, 9.

[11] Douglas Cowling, *Mr. Bach Comes to Call* (Ontario, Canada: The Children's Group, Inc., 1988), Track 12.

[12] Smith and Carlson, *The Gift of Music*, 32.

[13] Samuel Nisenson and William DeWitt, *Illustrated Minute Biographies* (New York, NY: Grosset & Dunlap, 1953), 19.

[14] Hans T. David and Arthur Mendel, *The Bach Reader: A Life of Johann Sebastian Bach in Letters & Documents* (New York, NY: W.W. Norton & Company, Inc., 1945), 47.

[15] Kavanaugh, *Spiritual Lives of the Great Composers*, 19.

[16] Thomas and Thomas, *Living Biographies of Great Composers*, 5.

[17] Ibid., 8.

[18] Krull, *Lives of the Musicians*, 17.

[19] Cynthia Millar, *Great Masters: Bach and His World* (Morristown, NJ: Silver Burdett Company, 1980), 13.

[20] David and Mendel, *The Bach Reader*, 288.

[21] Ibid., 336.

[22] Thomas and Thomas, *Living Biographies of Great Composers*, 4.

[23] Winter, *Sebastian*, 14.

[24] Smith and Carlson, *The Gift of Music*, 33.

[25] David and Mendel, *The Bach Reader*, 24. (An idea repeated in Smith and Carlson, *The Gift of Music*, 32.)

[26] Smith and Carlson, *The Gift of Music*, 33.

[27] Vernon, *Introducing Bach*, 30.

[28] Kavanaugh, *Spiritual Lives of Great Composers*, 17–18.

[29] Ibid., 20.

[30] Ibid., 22.

[31] Vernon, *Introducing Bach*, 5.

[32] Smith and Carlson, *The Gift of Music*, 33.

[33] Vernon, *Introducing Bach*, 31.
[34] David and Mendel, *The Bach Reader*, 287.
[35] Hendrik W. Van Loon, *The Life and Times of Johann Sebastian Bach* (London: George G. Harrap & Co. Ltd., 1942), no page number available.
[36] Vernon, *Introducing Bach*, 17.
[37] Krull, *Lives of the Musicians*, 15.
[38] Smith and Carlson, *The Gift of Music*, 33–34.
[39] Ibid., 35.
[40] Thomas and Thomas, *Living Biographies of Great Composers*, 4.
[41] Smith and Carlson, *The Gift of Music*, 34.
[42] Millar, *Great Masters*, 19.
[43] David and Mendel, *The Bach Reader*, 222.
[44] Ibid., 125.
[45] Nisenson and DeWitt, *Illustrated Minute Biographies*, 19.
[46] Smith and Carlson, *The Gift of Music*, 36.
[47] Millar, *Great Masters*, 25.
[48] Thomas and Thomas, *Living Biographies of Great Composers*, 8.
[49] Smith and Carlson, *The Gift of Music*, 34.